Graceful Beginnings
Short and Easy for Anyone New to the Bible

Painting the Portrait of Jesus

The "I AM" Word Pictures
Revealing the Jesus We Follow

MELANIE NEWTON

JOYFUL
WALK
BIBLE
STUDIES

Painting the Portrait of Jesus: The "I Am" Word Pictures Revealing the Jesus We Follow

© 2025 by Melanie Newton. All rights reserved.

Published by Joyful Walk Press. Flower Mound, TX.

ISBN: 979-8-9925750-8-8

For questions about the use of this study guide or for bulk orders, please email us at melanienewton.com/contact.

Cover photo by John Newton taken at Malleny Gardens, Balerno, Scotland, used by permission.

Melanie Newton is the author of "Graceful Beginnings" books for anyone new to the Bible and "Joyful Walk Bible Studies" for established Christians. Her mission is to help women learn to study the Bible for themselves and to grow their Bible-teaching skills to lead others.

Joyful Walk Bible Studies are grace-based studies for women of all ages. Each study guide follows the inductive method of Bible study (observation, interpretation, application) in a warm and inviting format.

We pray that you will find *Painting the Portrait of Jesus* to be a resource that God will use to strengthen you in your faith walk with Him.

Christ-Focused • Grace-Based • Bible-Rich

JOYFUL WALK PRESS
Flower Mound, TX

MELANIE NEWTON

Melanie Newton is a Louisiana girl who made the choice to follow Jesus while attending LSU. She and her husband Ron married and moved to Texas for him to attend Dallas Theological Seminary. They stayed in Texas where Ron led a wilderness camping ministry for troubled youth for many years. Ron now helps corporations with their challenging employees and is the author of the top-rated business book, *No Jerks on the Job*.

Melanie jumped into raising three Texas-born children and serving in ministry to women at her church. Through the years, the Lord has given her opportunity to do Bible teaching and to write grace-based Bible studies for women that are now available from her website (melanienewton.com) and on Bible.org. *Graceful Beginnings* books are for anyone new to the Bible. *Joyful Walk Bible Studies* are for maturing Christians.

Melanie Newton loves to help women learn how to study the Bible for themselves. She also teaches online courses for women to grow their Bible-teaching skills to help others—all with the goal of getting to know Jesus more along the way. Her heart's desire is to encourage you to have a joyful relationship with Jesus Christ so you are willing to share that experience with others around you.

"Jesus took hold of me in 1972, and I've been on this great adventure ever since. My life is a gift of God, full of blessings in the midst of difficult challenges. The more I've learned and experienced God's absolutely amazing grace, the more I've discovered my faith walk to be a joyful one. I'm still seeking that joyful walk every day..."

Melanie

OTHER BIBLE STUDIES BY MELANIE NEWTON

Graceful Beginnings Series books for anyone new to the Bible:

A Fresh Start (basics for new Christians)
Painting the Portrait of Jesus (the Gospel of John)
The God You Can Know (the character of God)
Grace Overflowing (an overview of Paul's 13 letters)
The Walk from Fear to Faith (7 Old Testament women)
Satisfied by His Love (women who knew Jesus)
Seek the Treasure (study of Ephesians)
Pathways to a Joyful Walk (6 pathways to a joy-filled life)

Joyful Walk Bible Studies for growing Christians:

Adorn Yourself with Godliness (1 Timothy and Titus, also in Spanish)
Everyday Women, Ever Faithful God (Old Testament women, also in Spanish)
Connecting Faith to Life on Planet Earth (Genesis 1-11; Revelation)
Graceful Living (the essentials for a grace-based Christian life)
Graceful Living Today (a devotional journal for a joyful life)
Healthy Living (Colossians and Philemon)
Heartbreak to Hope (the Gospel of Mark)
Identity: Sticking to Your Faith in a Pull-Apart World (Ezra thru Malachi)
Knowing Jesus, Knowing Joy (Philippians, also in Spanish)
Live Out His Love (New Testament women)
Perspective (1and 2 Thessalonians)
Profiles of Perseverance (Old Testament men, also in Spanish)
Radical Acts (Acts)
Reboot, Renew, Rejoice (1 and 2 Chronicles)
The God-Dependent Woman (2 Corinthians)
To Be Found Faithful (2 Timothy)

Resources for leading others

Be a Christ-Focused Small Group Leader
Leap into Lifestyle Disciplemaking
Bible Study Leadership Made Easy (online video course)
Painting the Picture of Jesus (The "I Am's" of Jesus for children)
Teaching Children the God They Can Know (the character of God)

Download our catalogue and get resources for your spiritual growth at melanienewton.com.

Contents

Introduction

GRACEFUL BEGINNINGS

The *Graceful Beginnings* books are Bible studies specifically designed for anyone new to the Bible—whether you are a new Christian or you just feel insecure about understanding the Bible. The short and easy lessons will introduce you to God and His way of approaching life in simple terms that can be easily understood.

Just as a newborn baby needs to know the love and trustworthiness of her parents, the new Christian needs to know and experience the love and trustworthiness of her God. *A Fresh Start* is the first book in the series, laying a good foundation of truth for you to grasp and apply to your life. The other books in the series can be done in any order.

SOME BIBLE BASICS

Throughout these lessons, you will use a Bible to answer questions as you discover treasure about your life with Christ. The Bible is one book containing a collection of 66 books combined together for our benefit. It is divided into two main parts: the Old Testament and the New Testament.

The Old Testament tells the story of the beginning of the world and God's promises to mankind given through the nation of Israel. It tells how the people of Israel obeyed and disobeyed God over many, many years. All the stories and messages in the Old Testament lead up to Jesus Christ's coming to the earth.

The New Testament tells the story of Jesus Christ, the early Christians, and God's promises to all those who believe in Jesus. You can think of the Old Testament as "before Christ" and the New Testament as "after Christ."

Each book of the Bible is divided into chapters and verses within those chapters to make it easier to study. Bible references include the book name, chapter number and verse number(s). For example, Ephesians 2:8 refers to the New Testament book of Ephesians, the 2nd chapter, and verse 8 within that 2nd chapter. Printed Bibles have a "Table of Contents" in the front to help you locate books by page number. Bible apps also have a contents list by book and chapter.

The Bible verses highlighted at the beginning of each lesson in this study are from the New International Version® (NIV®) unless otherwise indicated. You can use any version of the Bible to answer the questions, but using a more easy-to-read translation (NIRV, NLT, NIV, NET, ESV) will help you gain confidence in understanding what you are reading. You can find all these translations in the YouVersion App, the Blue Letter Bible App, or at biblegateway.com.

This study capitalizes certain pronouns referring to God, Jesus and the Holy Spirit—He, Him, His, Himself—just to make the reading of the study information less confusing. Some Bible translations likewise capitalize those pronouns referring to God; others do not. It is simply a matter of preference, not a requirement.

PAINTING THE PORTRAIT OF JESUS

The *Painting the Portrait of Jesus* lessons focus on what are commonly called the "I Am's." The "I Am's" are statements that Jesus made in the gospel of John (the fourth book of the New Testament). They are called the "I Am's" because each one of them starts with the same 2 words, "I am." Then, Jesus follows the words "I am" with a phrase to describe Himself to those who are listening.

As one who lived as a man among us, He understands the spiritual needs of men, women, boys, and girls. These "I am" declarations are like colors Jesus used for the canvas of His own self-portrait so His followers could know Him better and understand His significance in their lives. These "colors" reveal the Jesus that we follow. And studying them is in a sense "Painting the Portrait of Jesus."

Here's what you are going to learn in the *Painting the Portrait of Jesus* lessons—**Jesus is the answer to the spiritual needs of every person.** He is the answer to every inner need that you have. And you will see that His self-portrait describes that.

With each lesson, you'll be adding to your portrait of Jesus as you study the "I Am's." As He reveals Himself, you will long for a close relationship with this same Jesus, the one to whom you belong. And you will want to **follow** Him because He is trustworthy!

Jesus offers you a new life that is joyful and fruitful. Following Him involves trusting Him to guide you in your daily life through what you read in God's Word and through talking to God. You can enjoy a relationship with Him—now and forever!

ELEMENTS OF EACH LESSON

This book covers the "I Am's" of Jesus in 8 lessons.

1. Each lesson begins with a Bible verse that relates to the focus of the lesson. We recommend that you memorize these verses as they are easy ones for you to learn. The point is to begin the habit of memorizing Scripture. You will be surprised at how soon it just flows from your mind.

2. Start your study with the prayer given after the focus Bible verse. Prayer is just talking to God as conversation with someone who loves you dearly. The beginning prayer simply asks Jesus to teach you through the lesson.

3. This is followed by a simple study of the verses being covered by the lesson. Read the Bible verses and answer the associated questions. This study uses the NIV translation. We recommend you use that or other easy-to-read translations (CSB, NLT, NET, ESV). See "Bible Basics" above for online sources of these.

4. In the "Following Jesus" section at the end of the study questions, you will be encouraged to dwell more on what you learned in the lesson that applies to following Jesus. This will also include times of reflection and prayer.

5. Deeper Discoveries (optional): We have provided additional reading of the book of John. You can spend a few minutes reading and reflecting on what you learn about who Jesus is and why you can trust Him with your life.

SMALL GROUP DISCUSSION

While you can work through these lessons as a personal study, this study is perfect to use for small groups. Share the following suggested guidelines with the group members to maximize your discussion group experience.

• Set aside some time each week to do the study questions so that you will get to know God better.

• Consistently attend whether your lesson is done or not. You will learn from the discussion.

- Respect each other's insights. Listen thoughtfully. Share your own insights, but do not dominate the discussion.

- Celebrate unity in Christ by avoiding controversial subjects such as politics, divisive issues and denominational differences.

- Maintain confidentiality of whatever is shared within the group.

Enjoy your small group discussion and learn from one another. As you do so, you will have a greater connection with each other. And you'll have more reason to praise our God as you see and hear how He has been faithful to each of you through the years. A small group is a great place to share how you are following Jesus in your life.

SUGGESTED LEADER GUIDE FOR GROUP DISCUSSION:

Discussing the lesson (apart from the "Deeper Discoveries" readings) should take about an hour, making this an easy study to fit into a busy workday schedule.

Go to my website, melanienewton.com/john to download a more detailed discussion guide for this study. Or follow the suggestions below:

1. Pray for the Lord Jesus to teach you what He wants you to know through the lesson.

2. Work through the LESSON together, reading the Bible verses and discussing the questions. Predetermine which of the explanatory paragraphs you will read as a group. Most simply confirm the truths learned in the questions just asked.

3. Read the "FOLLOWING JESUS" section and share responses to any included application questions.

4. Pray for the group members using the prayer prompts at the end of the lesson.

5. Remind each person to do the next lesson before the group meets again.

Overview of the "I Am's"

✓ White represents the presence of God. JESUS IS THE "I AM." He is the answer to the spiritual needs of every person.

Jesus answered, "Before Abraham was born, I am." (John 8:58)

✓ Purple represents abundance & being satisfied. JESUS IS THE BREAD OF LIFE. His abundant love satisfies our hunger for a relationship with God.

Then Jesus declared, "I am the bread of life. Whoever comes to me will never go hungry, and whoever believes in me will never be thirsty." (John 6:35)

✓ Yellow represents light & guidance. JESUS IS THE LIGHT OF THE WORLD. His light directs us to follow Him.

When Jesus spoke again to the people, he said, "I am the light of the world. Whoever follows me will never walk in darkness, but will have the light of life." (John 8:12)

✓ Orange represents safety. JESUS IS THE GATE FOR THE SHEEP. There is safety in following Jesus and doing life His way.

Very truly I tell you, I am the gate for the sheep...whoever enters through me will be saved. They will come in and go out, and find pasture. (John 10:7,9)

✓ Green represents relationship. JESUS IS THE GOOD SHEPHERD. You can enjoy a forever relationship with Him.

I am the good shepherd. The good shepherd lays down his life for the sheep...I am the good shepherd. I know my sheep, and my sheep know me. (John 10:11, 14)

✓ Blue represents the hope of eternal life. JESUS IS THE RESURRECTION AND THE LIFE. To His followers He gives eternal spiritual life now and eternal physical life in a new body after death.

Jesus said to her, "I am the resurrection and the life. The one who believes in me will live, even though they die; and whoever lives by believing in me will never die. Do you believe this?" (John 11:25)

✓ Red represents love, life, and celebration. JESUS IS THE WAY, THE TRUTH, AND THE LIFE. He gives us His life so that we are completely loved and accepted by God our Father. Celebrate!

Jesus answered, "I am the way and the truth and the life. No one comes to the Father except through me." (John 14:6)

✓ Brown represents nourishment to bear fruit. JESUS IS THE VINE. He nourishes us with His life so we can bear fruit in our lives that represents our connection with Him.

I am the vine. You are the branches. If you remain in me, and I in you, you will bear much fruit; apart from me you can do nothing. (John 15:5)

Jesus painted Himself with words that reveal a "picture" of who He is, how He meets our needs, and why we can trust Him enough to follow Him.

Enjoy!

Jesus Is the "I Am"

*Jesus answered, "Before Abraham was born, **I AM.**" (John 8:58)*

> **Pray:** Lord Jesus, please teach me through this lesson.

Have you ever worked on a paint-by-number or color-by-number picture? How easy is it to tell what the picture is before you paint or color it? For some, you can look at it and guess what the picture might be. For others, you can't really tell what it is. So, what do you need to do to start finding out what the picture will really look like? If you are like most people, you usually start with one number that represents one color and fill in all the spaces having that number with the appropriate color. After you've colored in that number, the picture begins to be revealed. Then, you do the same with the other colors. After adding each color to the picture, you can finally recognize what the picture represents. You get the complete picture.

You can also paint a picture with words.

> *Think about 3 words true about you that you could use to describe yourself.*

> *Now say, "I am..." followed by those three words.*

You just painted a picture of yourself with those words. That's similar to what Jesus did with statements that He made about Himself in the gospel of John. These statements are called the "I am's" because each one of them starts with the same 2 words, "I am." Then, Jesus follows the words "I am" with a word picture to describe Himself to those who are listening.

Just like adding each color to a paint-by-number picture enables you to recognize the picture, Jesus used the "I Am" descriptions to paint His own portrait.

A portrait is a *painting, drawing, or photograph of a person.* Usually, a portrait reveals someone's physical appearance—the true likeness of that person. When you look in a mirror, you see a likeness of yourself. In a sense that's a portrait.

Jesus' portrait does not reveal His physical appearance. Instead, Jesus did what I asked you to do above—describe yourself with a few words to "paint" a portrait of yourself. Each one of those "I am" statements is like another paint color being added to Jesus' portrait.

Jesus painted Himself with word pictures to describe Himself to those who were listening. These word pictures reveal not His physical appearance but a "picture" of who He is and the difference He could make in the lives of those who trust in Him enough to follow Him. Discovering these truths will make a difference in your life as well.

Jesus is the answer to the spiritual needs of every person. He is the answer to every inner need that you and I have. And you will see that His self-portrait describes that. We'll be adding a different color each lesson as we paint the portrait of Jesus.

PAINT COLOR #1: WHITE

Our first paint color is white. White is really a mixture of all colors. Have you ever seen white light shining through a prism?

A prism is a special kind of glass that causes white light shining through it to break up into all the different colors of a rainbow. All those colors miraculously mix together to form white light. So, white represents all the colors Jesus used to paint His portrait. And in the Bible, the color white often represents **the presence of God**.

We find the "I am" statements in the book of John, written by one of Jesus' disciples named John. The book of John is also called the gospel of John. The word "gospel" means "good news" so the book of John contains the good news about Jesus—who He is, why He came, and what He offers to those who trust in Him. In it, John emphasizes this truth: **The invisible God can be seen and known through His Son, Jesus Christ.** We see this truth in the key verse for the book of John found in chapter 20.

Read John 20:31.

John wrote so the reader would believer what?

And once you know and believe this, what will you have?

The New International Readers Version says it this way, "You will have life because you belong to Him." Belonging to Him means you will have a relationship with Him. It's great to belong to someone who loves you, isn't it? And once you belong to Him, you also get life from Him, eternal life. We'll learn a lot about both of these special things that come to those who know that Jesus is God's Son and believe that to be true.

Let's talk about the two words "I am." To us, they are just part of our English language. To the Jewish people of Jesus' time, those words were part of God's name. Years before Jesus was born, God spoke to a man named Moses and told Moses to lead the people of Israel out of Egypt. Moses said to God, "What if I go to them, and they want to know your name, what shall I tell them?" We read God's answer in Exodus chapter 3.

Read Exodus 3:13-14.

What name did God give Himself?

That's what our English Bibles say. The Old Testament where Exodus is found was written in the Hebrew language. The Hebrew name for God is spelled YHWH. We think the name was pronounced Yahweh (yaway). This was God's personal name. Jesus knew this name for God. And He frequently claimed that name for Himself.

One time, Jesus was talking to a woman at a well. She said that one future day the promised leader known as the Messiah would come. Let's see how Jesus answered her.

Read John 4:19-26.

What would the Messiah do when He comes (v. 25)?

How did Jesus respond to her (v. 26)?

Since Jesus spoke Hebrew, what He originally said would have been, "Yahweh, the one speaking to you."

What was Jesus communicating to the woman about Himself?

Another time, Jesus was talking to some Jewish leaders and told them He knew Abraham. They said, "You are not even 50 years old. How could you have seen Abraham?" Let's see how Jesus answered them.

Read John 8:56-59.

What was Jesus' answer in v. 58?

Notice what happened next. Why did the Jewish leaders become so angry with Jesus?

So, this is what you can know. When Jesus said, "I am," He is revealing something about Himself. He is God. He did the things that God does. He healed people and forgave them of their sins. He told people that He was God. **Jesus is the "I am."** He is God.

We don't think of God's name as Yahweh anymore. We often think of God's name as Jesus, don't we? The New Testament refers to Him as the Lord Jesus Christ. Jesus is the name given to Him at birth by the angel. Christ is His title (from Greek *christos*, which translates the Hebrew title "Messiah"). Lord refers to His being God.

Remember that I told you the color white represents the presence of God. One day, when Jesus was on a mountain with His disciples, His clothes became dazzlingly white, whiter than any washing product they had could ever make them. His disciples saw that and knew it meant they were in God's presence.

Read Mark 9:2-8.

What did the disciples hear the voice from heaven say?

So, not only is Jesus God, He is more specifically the Son of God. He knows God as His very own Father.

Jesus obeyed His Father and lived His life as a God-man among people. That way, He knows every need that we have—every need, both physical and spiritual. He knows what it is like to be hungry and thirsty, to know fear, to be alone, and to long to know God.

Jesus knows that He is the answer to every need, especially the need to know God.

Read Hebrews 4:15-16.

What is true about Jesus as your High Priest (representative before God) in v. 15?

When we go to Him, what will you receive (v. 16)?

As fully God and fully human, you can be confident that Jesus understands how you feel. And Jesus is powerful enough (as God) to take care of your every need. **Jesus is the "I AM."** He said to His disciples, "If you know me, you will know God." That's what Jesus is saying to you and what the rest of these lessons will be about—getting to know Jesus through His descriptions of Himself as though they were paint colors. With that we'll paint the portrait of Jesus.

Jesus is the answer to the spiritual needs of every person, especially the need to have a relationship with Him, to belong to Someone who loves you dearly.

FOLLOWING JESUS

Read Matthew 11:28-30.

What is the invitation and the promise?

Have you accepted Jesus' invitation to come to Him in faith?

What inner needs do you have that Jesus' promise could satisfy?

Isn't it great to know that you are loved by someone as wonderful as Jesus? Through faith in Him, you are completely accepted and loved by God your Father. And you can enjoy awesome treasures God promises to you.

Jesus offers you a new life that is joyful and fruitful. Following Him involves trusting Him to guide you in your daily life through what you read in God's Word and through talking to God.

You can enjoy a relationship with Him—now and forever!

> **Pray:** *Thank Jesus for coming to earth and living among us so that you can see what God is like by learning from Him. Thank Him that He wants to have a relationship with you. Ask Him to give you a longing in your heart this week to know Him closely.*

DEEPER DISCOVERIES (OPTIONAL):

Like Matthew, Mark, and Luke, the gospel of John contains the good news about Jesus—who He is, why He came, and what He offers to those who trust in Him. Spend a few minutes each day reading the verses and reflecting on Jesus—His life, His relationships, and His teaching. Get to know Him well—this One who loves you dearly.

Read John 1:1-28. Reflect on what you read.

Read John 1:29-51. Reflect on what you read.

Read John 2:1-12. Reflect on what you read.

Read John 2:13-25. Reflect on what you read.

Jesus Is the Bread of Life

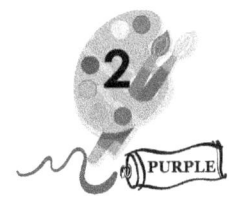

*Then Jesus declared, "**I am the bread of life.** Whoever comes to me will never go hungry, and whoever believes in me will never be thirsty." (John 6:35)*

Pray: Lord Jesus, please teach me through this lesson.

PAINTING THE PORTRAIT OF JESUS

✓ JESUS IS THE "I AM." He is the answer to the spiritual needs of every person. *John 8:58*

PAINT COLOR #2: PURPLE

Today, we are painting with the color "purple."

What does the color purple mean to you, or what do you associate with the color purple?

Throughout history, the color purple has often been associated with kings, queens and other very rich people. Kings and emperors dressed in purple clothing to display their importance because purple dye was quite expensive. Only the wealthy could afford to have clothes dyed with purple. So, purple as a color represents **abundance**—having plenty of everything, including food so that your hunger is being **satisfied**.

Consider the word satisfied. What does it mean to be satisfied?

Give examples of feeling satisfied because of having abundance.

One day Jesus saw a huge crowd of people coming towards Him as He was teaching. He knew they would be hungry so His disciples found a boy with 5 small loaves of bread and 2 small fish. That's all Jesus needed to feed the crowd of more than 5000. Do you remember what happened?

Read John 6:5-15.

If you were a reporter, what parts of this event would really stand out to you so that you would write about it?

Did you notice that Jesus fed every one of those people as much as they wanted to eat so that they were **satisfied** (v. 11)? For that day, at least, they were satisfied.

The next day, the crowd was hungry again so they searched for Jesus. When they found Him, Jesus fussed at them because they were only looking for Him to give them more food, not to believe in Him as the Son of God. He said they should not be hungry just for physical food but for the bread that comes down from heaven to give life to the world.

Read John 6:25-34.

When they asked Jesus what work they must do to please God (vv. 28-29), how did Jesus answer?

What kind of bread were the people thinking Jesus was offering to them (vv. 30-31)?

Read John 6:35.

How did Jesus answer them?

Have you ever gone without eating for a whole day or longer? What was that like?

Without food, your body begins to get weaker. Food is one of our basic needs; we all must eat to live.

In most of the countries of the world, the main food source for people is bread made from some kind of flour. That's been true for the past 4000 years or so. People have eaten bread for breakfast, lunch, and dinner along with some other things like cheese and fruit. To them, bread means life. Without it, they starve. When their grain crops fail because of drought or disease, they have no bread. That was true for the people in Jesus' crowd. There were no grocery stores.

Today, we don't depend on just bread in America (or in your country) because we have so many different kinds of food. But we still need food to live, whether bread or not, so food sustains life. Jesus was telling the crowd that He is even more important to them than their daily meals.

Reread John 6:35.

What does Jesus promise to those who come to Him?

Did Jesus mean that once you believe in Him you don't have to eat food or drink water every day? See v. 27.

Jesus meant something else. During this story in John chapter 6, Jesus says 6 times that He is the bread who came down from heaven to give life to the world (vv. 33, 38, 41, 50, 51, & 58).

Since bread is usually meant to be eaten, that means you must personally take it into your body so that it nourishes you for life. That's physical bread giving physical life. Jesus refers to Himself as spiritual bread that gives spiritual life through a relationship with God.

What invitation does Jesus give in John 6:35 to satisfy your spiritual hunger?

God creates every human with a hunger for a relationship with Him.

Before knowing Christ, how did you try to satisfy that hunger?

How can you satisfy that hunger now?

Sometimes people try to satisfy that hunger by staying very busy or doing good works or following a set of rules. The Jewish people followed many rules. But Jesus didn't say, "I am the bread of life. He who completely follows the rules will never go hungry again." The food the Jesus gives to satisfy our spiritual hunger will never spoil. He will never run out of it. That's **abundance**.

And He makes another promise to everyone who comes to Him.

Read John 6:36-37.

What does Jesus say He will never do?

Isn't that wonderful? He wants you to be close to Him, and He will never reject you. He will never push you away. That's eternal life. And His love for you is **abundant** and **satisfying**.

You will not feel hungry for God's love because you will have it constantly. Have you experienced that?

Jesus is our bread of life. His abundant love satisfies our hunger for a relationship with God.

FOLLOWING JESUS

Next time you have lunch or dinner, think about how that never lasts long. You always get hungry again. But Jesus said if you come to Him for your spiritual food, He will **satisfy** the hunger in your heart for a relationship with the God who made you.

Think about it, where in your life do you not feel satisfied?

So, the question to ask is this, "How do I go to Jesus for spiritual food so that I can be satisfied?"

- First, you get your spiritual needs satisfied by trusting in Him to take away your sins. You only need to do this once in your life. After you have done that…

- Follow Him every day by reading your Bible, especially the parts that talk about Jesus—the books called Matthew, Mark, Luke and John. Those will tell you all about who Jesus is. The "Deeper Discoveries" section at the end of each lesson suggests that you read through the book of John, a couple of chapters at a time.

- Talk to Him through prayer. Prayer is simply conversation with Someone who loves you dearly. Jesus is always there for you. Will you do that this week?

> **Pray:** Talk to Jesus about any feelings of spiritual hunger or thirst that you might have. Tell Him you are ready to begin to experience being satisfied by His abundant love that He gives to those who come to Him and follow Him.

DEEPER DISCOVERIES (OPTIONAL):

Spend a few minutes each day reading the verses and reflecting on Jesus—His life, His relationships, and His teaching. Get to know Him well—this One who loves you dearly.

Read John 3:1-21. Reflect on what you read.

Read John 3:22-36. Reflect on what you read.

Read John 4:1-26. Reflect on what you read.

Read John 4:27-54. Reflect on what you read.

Jesus Is the Light of the World

*When Jesus spoke again to the people, he said, "**I am the light of the world.** Whoever follows me will never walk in darkness, but will have the light of life." (John 8:12)*

Pray: Lord Jesus, please teach me through this lesson.

PAINTING THE PORTRAIT OF JESUS

✓ JESUS IS THE "I AM." He is the answer to the spiritual needs of every person. *John 8:58*

✓ JESUS IS THE BREAD OF LIFE. His abundant love satisfies our hunger for a relationship with God. *John 6:35*

PAINT COLOR #3: YELLOW

Today's paint color is yellow since we'll be talking about light. Would you agree that the sun is the biggest yellow object you know? Bright sunlight warms us up and helps us to see the world around us. At night, the sun is shining on the other side of the earth so it is dark here. When it's dark, you might feel afraid or alone. You might feel confused because you cannot see where to go. You can stumble and fall without light to guide you.

Light helps us to see where we are going so we can keep going in the right **direction** and not get lost. Think of how a light at the end of a dark hallway **directs** you to the doorway so you don't keep bumping into the walls. So, for this lesson the color yellow represents **light** and **direction**.

In our world, we depend on electricity to give us light in the dark. Just turn on a lamp or a switch and get instant light. When Jesus lived on the earth, there was no electricity. People depended on candles and oil lamps for light at night. Imagine what it would have been like to look out your window at night without any streetlights—anywhere! Consider how dark it could have been.

If you have been in a very dark place, what was that like?

How does darkness make you feel?

Jesus understood how much we need light to **direct** us in the darkness. One day He was attending a festival in Jerusalem during the fall. A major part of that festival was the lighting of huge lamps that lit up the entire temple area. Those weren't the small oil lamps most people owned. They were really big ones that shone light all over the temple building. The people would gather together in that light to sing praises to God and dance. Right in the middle of that time of singing and dancing, Jesus told the crowd something about Himself.

Read John 8:12.

What does Jesus call Himself?

What is the promise to those who follow Jesus?

You already thought about darkness and how it makes you feel. Sometimes scared, sometimes confused, and sometimes lonely. When there's darkness all around us, light gives us **direction** to follow the right path. Light gives us security and makes us feel less lonely. Light helps us to see clearly.

Suppose I turned on a flashlight and pointed it at various objects in a dark room while asking you "What do you see?" After looking at several objects and hearing your responses, I could ask, "How did you know what I wanted you to see?" You would probably answer that the light directed your eyes. The light helped you to see each object better. Light gives us **direction**.

> *What do you think Jesus meant when He said He was the light of the world? (Consider the flashlight example above.)*

Darkness in the Bible usually means not knowing God and His love. But Jesus promises His light leads to life. Life in the Bible means spiritual life—knowing God and His wonderful love for us and living a life that pleases God. Light gives us **direction**. So, our yellow paint represents both **light** and **direction**. That's what Jesus said about Himself in John 8:12.

Not too long after Jesus made that announcement to the crowd, Jesus was in Jerusalem walking around. As Jesus went along, He saw a man who was born blind. That man had never seen the sun or the sky. You might know someone who is blind. Most of the time people who are blind can't see any light at all. They are always in the dark.

> *If you couldn't see with your eyes, what would you miss the most?*

Read John 9:1-7.

> *What did Jesus' disciples think was the reason the man had been born blind (v. 2)? [Note: That's what many people of Jesus' day thought.]*

What was Jesus' response (v. 3)?

God wasn't angry with the man and punishing him. God allowed this man to be born blind for a special purpose. Then Jesus said these words again, "**I am the light of the world (v. 5).**"

What did Jesus do next (vv. 6-7)?

What happened then (v. 7)?

How do you think the man felt to at last be able to see?

Read John 9:8-34.

How did other people who knew the blind man respond to the knowledge of his being healed?

vv. 8-12—

vv. 13-17—

vv. 18-23—

vv. 24-34—

The blind man's neighbors could hardly believe it. They kept saying, "Isn't this the same man who used to sit and beg?" Some said, "Yes." Others said, "No. He only looks like him." But the man who had been blind, let's call him the ex-blind man, kept saying, "I am the man. The man they call Jesus made some mud and put it on my eyes. He told me to go…and wash. So I went and washed. Then I could see." But the ex-blind man didn't know what Jesus looked like or where He was.

Some of the Jewish leaders who didn't believe in Jesus found out what happened to the man. Instead of praising God for the healing, they refused to believe that Jesus was God. And they got angry with the ex-blind man and threw him out of their church building!

Read John 9:35-39.

When Jesus heard that the Jewish leaders had thrown the ex-blind man out, what did He do and say (v. 35)? [Note: "Son of Man" was something Jesus called Himself.}

How did the ex-blind man answer (v. 36)?

When Jesus revealed Himself, how did the ex-blind man respond (v. 38)?

How did Jesus as light of the world give light to the blind man?

How do you think the man's life changed after this?

FOLLOWING JESUS

To follow Jesus means to believe in Him, trust what He says, and trust what He tells us to do in the Bible.

In what areas of your life do you need light and direction?

What do you think it would look like to follow Jesus in those areas?

Jesus is the light of the world. His light directs us to follow Him. And when you follow Jesus, you are never alone because He is always with you, just like turning on a lamp in a dark room makes you feel less lonely.

No one can put out the light that Jesus brings into the world. Praise God for that!

> **Pray:** Are you willing to trust Jesus as the light of your life and follow Him this week? Go ahead and talk to Him about how to follow Him in your life today.

DEEPER DISCOVERIES (OPTIONAL):

Spend a few minutes each day reading the verses below and reflecting on Jesus—His life, His relationships, and His teaching. Get to know Him well—this One who loves you dearly.

Read John 5:1-30. Reflect on what you read.

Read John 5:31-47. Reflect on what you read.

Read John 6:1-24. Reflect on what you read.

Read John 6:25-71. Reflect on what you read.

Jesus Is the Gate for the Sheep

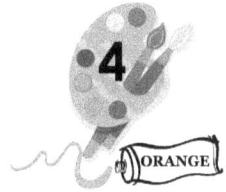

*Very truly I tell you, **I am the gate for the sheep**...whoever enters through me will be saved. They will come in and go out, and find pasture. (John 10:7, 9)*

Pray: Lord Jesus, please teach me through this lesson.

PAINTING THE PORTRAIT OF JESUS

✓ JESUS IS THE "I AM." He is the answer to the spiritual needs of every person. *John 8:58*

✓ JESUS IS THE BREAD OF LIFE. His abundant love satisfies our hunger for a relationship with God. *John 6:35*

✓ JESUS IS THE LIGHT OF THE WORLD. His light directs us to follow Him. *John 8:12*

PAINT COLOR #4: ORANGE

The color in this lesson is orange—a color often associated with **safety**. You may have seen a highway construction worker wearing an orange vest. Highway workers also use orange cones and barrels to tell the driver which lanes are open and which are closed for repairs. In fact, the shade of orange used is called "Safety Orange." The United States government requires that certain construction equipment must be painted "safety orange." So, what does "Safety Orange" have to do with Jesus?

In John chapter 10, Jesus described Himself as a shepherd for sheep. It is common in the Bible for kings and priests and other leaders to consider themselves shepherds of the people, their sheep. In this lesson, we'll learn what it means when Jesus called Himself a gate for the sheep. In the next lesson, we'll cover Jesus as the good shepherd.

Read John 10:1-10.

How does Jesus describe Himself in vv. 7 and 9?

You might be thinking, "That sounds weird. Why does Jesus call Himself a gate or door? What does a gate have to do with being a shepherd?" Actually, it made a lot of sense to the people listening to Him.

Every community would have a sheep pen with high walls and one doorway. Some countries today still have these kinds of sheep pens. Several flocks of sheep would go in the sheep pen at night to keep them from wandering and getting lost. The sheep inside the walls would be **kept safe** from wolves and thieves who tried to break in and steal them. A watchman would guard the opening all night long.

Here's what happened every day if you were a sheep. In the morning, you and your sheep friends see the shepherds come through the doorway to get their sheep. As the shepherds are calling out to their sheep, you hear your own shepherd's voice calling the special name he's given to you. Yay! You run on your little sheep legs to where he is. He leads you and your flock mates out of the sheep pen. Then, he leads the flock to the pastures. You follow close behind him.

Once you get to the pastures, you see a small fenced area. The shepherd takes his place in the doorway or entrance of the fenced area and functions as a door or gate. You can **safely** go out and munch on grass for as long as you want because your shepherd is watching over you. But if you get tired or frightened, you can go into the fenced area where it is **safe** and secure. Your shepherd is still watching over you. He is the gate.

Reread John 10:9.

> *Look again at what Jesus said He does as the gate. What does Jesus promise to anyone who enters through Him as the gate?*

See that phrase "will be **saved**?" The Bible teaches that every person needs to be saved because of sin. Remember that God loves everyone. But every person has done bad things called sin. God says that sin separates us from Him forever. He didn't want that to happen so He sent His Son Jesus to take the punishment for your sin and my sin so we don't have to be separated from God forever.

When you trust in Jesus and what He did to take away your sin, you are **saved**. You are saved from being separated from God, and you are saved from being punished for your sin. That's what it means to be **saved**.

When Jesus says, "Anyone who enters through me will be saved," He was telling the people that anyone who trusts in Him will be **saved** from being separated from God forever.

> *What can the sheep do within this "safety" zone (second part of v. 9)?*

Being able to come and go to find pasture presents a picture of freedom and fulfillment, doesn't it? Jesus offers that to us as His sheep as well.

The phrase "will be saved" can also be translated "be **kept safe.**" To those who already trust in Jesus and are already following Jesus like sheep follow their shepherd, Jesus promises to **keep you safe**. Now, people are not really sheep. But every person needs to feel safe. There are enemies out there who want to hurt Jesus' sheep.

Reread John 10:10.

> *What do the enemies (such as a thief) want to do to the sheep?*

> *That's not good for sheep, is it? What does Jesus promise His sheep?*

What does it mean to have an abundant or full life, one that is rich and satisfying?

Abundant life is life that is so satisfying that it is like a cup overflowing. That's better than any sheep could ever imagine. As a follower of Jesus, He promises you life that is full and satisfying. The Bible calls it eternal life. We sometimes think it only starts when we die and go to be with Jesus in heaven. But you have eternal life while you are here on earth, too.

Jesus is the gate for the sheep. There is safety in following Jesus and doing life His way.

FOLLOWING JESUS

This life with God that Jesus provides for you is good and satisfying. You only need to follow Him to enjoy it here. Notice that Jesus said He was the gate for the sheep, not the jail keeper. ☺

Reread John 10:9.

Why should you consider Jesus to be someone who offers you freedom to live a fulfilling life rather than someone who is restrictive?

Following Jesus' way of doing life can help to keep you safe from enemies in your life. What other voices try to get you to follow them?

What would it look like to follow Jesus as your shepherd rather than those who keep you from following Him?

You can feel safe in Jesus' loving arms knowing He cares so much for you and is watching over you while you enjoy the freedom He provides.

> **Pray:** Ask Jesus to direct you to His way of doing life. Thank Him for watching over you while you enjoy the freedom He provides.

DEEPER DISCOVERIES (OPTIONAL):

Spend a few minutes each day reading the verses below and reflecting on Jesus—His life, His relationships, and His teaching. Get to know Him well—this One who loves you dearly.

Read John 7:1-24. Reflect on what you read.

John 7:25-53. Reflect on what you read.

Read John 8:1-30. Reflect on what you read.

Read John 8:31-59. Reflect on what you read.

Jesus Is the Good Shepherd

I am the good shepherd. The good shepherd lays down his life for the sheep...I am the good shepherd. I know my sheep, and my sheep know me. (John 10:11, 14)

Pray: Lord Jesus, please teach me through this lesson.

PAINTING THE PORTRAIT OF JESUS

✓ JESUS IS THE "I AM." He is the answer to the spiritual needs of every person. *John 8:58*

✓ JESUS IS THE BREAD OF LIFE. His abundant love satisfies our hunger for a relationship with God. *John 6:35*

✓ JESUS IS THE LIGHT OF THE WORLD. His light directs us to follow Him. *John 8:12*

✓ JESUS IS THE GATE FOR THE SHEEP. There is safety in following Jesus and doing life His way. *John 10:7, 9*

PAINT COLOR #5: GREEN

Our color for this lesson is green. We're going to learn about Jesus as a shepherd again. It makes sense to choose green to represent all the good grass the shepherd provides for the sheep to eat. But green is also associated with peacefulness and rest. Jesus told His followers, "Come to me and I will give you rest (Matthew 11:28-29)." So, green will represent **relationship**. We can enjoy a **relationship** with Jesus as our shepherd. We can **know** and **belong** to Him as His sheep. This satisfies our need for a relationship with our God.

In the last lesson, we learned that Jesus told His followers that He was a gate of protection for His sheep. Let's find out more about Jesus as a shepherd.

Read John 10:11-15.

What does Jesus call himself in vv. 11 and 14?

Do you think every sheep wants a good shepherd?

Jesus described Himself as the good shepherd who does what for the sheep (vv. 11, 15)?

What could it mean for a shepherd to give his life for his sheep?

As Jesus was talking to His followers, He knew that their greatest enemy was being separated from God because of sin in their lives.

Jesus gave His life for us, His sheep, when He took the punishment for sin by dying on the cross. He did this so that anyone who trusts in Him will have all of their sins forgiven, will receive eternal life, and will never be separated from God again.

But that's not the only way **Jesus is the Good Shepherd**. Look at what else He says. *"I know my sheep, and my sheep know me (v. 14)."* That's all about relationship. **Jesus wants us to enjoy a personal relationship with Him.**

Shepherds of Jesus' time were devoted to their sheep. They talked to them and even sang to them. The shepherd cared so much for every sheep in his flock that he gave a special name to each one.

So, if you were a sheep in the sheep pen, not only would you hear the sound of the shepherd's voice, you would also hear him calling your name. We mentioned that in the last lesson.

Read John 10:3-4.

The shepherd calls out to the sheep. What is the responsibility of the sheep?

The shepherd calls those sheep who belong to Him. Jesus knows every one of us who have believed in Him and trusted in Him to take away our sins. He knows each one of His followers by name. We each have a personal **relationship** with Jesus, our shepherd.

Not only do we have a relationship with Jesus, it's a **forever relationship**. It is one we can never lose. He will never turn His back on His sheep. We belong to Him, and He belongs to us. Read with me what He says about our security in Him

Read John 10:27-30.

What does Jesus give to His followers (v. 28)?

When Jesus said, "they will never die," He did not mean that your body will not grow old and die. In the last lesson, you learned that you don't have to wait until you die to get eternal life. Eternal life begins the moment you trust in Jesus to take away your sins.

If you are Jesus' sheep, who can steal you out of His hand (v. 28)?

So, does that mean you will always belong to Him?

Can there be a time in the future when you don't belong to Him?

*There isn't anything that can make you not **belong** to Jesus any more. You are in a forever **relationship** with Him as His sheep. That is great news, isn't it?*

When Jesus talks about His father, He is talking about God. The Bible teaches that there is one God who exists in three persons. God the Father, God the Son, and God the Holy Spirit. When Jesus says, "My Father," He's talking about God the Father. Jesus is His Son, so Jesus is God the Son.

According to Jesus' words (v. 29), who is greater than anyone?

Can someone take you out of God the Father's hands?

Is anyone stronger or more powerful than God?

Are you more powerful than God?

So, once you trust in Jesus to take away your sin and become one of Jesus' followers, one of His sheep, is there anything you can do to make yourself not belong to God any longer?

Remember this. It's not the sheep that are holding onto the shepherd. If you have ever seen a sheep, you know they are not very strong creatures. It is the power of the shepherd holding onto the sheep.

Jesus knows that His followers are not as strong as He is. You **belong** to Jesus forever because of His powerful grip holding onto you.

How does knowing that truth make you feel?

Read Romans 8:38-39.

What additional confirmation about God's hold onto you do you get from these verses?

The Bible teaches that nothing that happens during your lifetime, nothing that happens after you die, nothing that you do right now, and nothing that you do in the future can separate you from Jesus.

FOLLOWING JESUS

If you are already one of Jesus' sheep, **you are in a forever relationship with Him.** God continually loves you until the day your body dies, and then God continually loves you afterwards as you live in heaven with Him.

So, if a family member says to you, "You are not perfect. I saw you do something wrong. Surely God doesn't love you anymore." How do you answer that?

If you trusted Christ to take away your sin last year, and someone says to you, "Well, you've done some bad things since then. You do not belong to Jesus anymore." How do you answer that?

If you dream about something evil taking you away from Jesus, of what should you remind yourself when you awake?

Jesus is the good shepherd. We can enjoy a forever **relationship** with Him. Once you trust in Christ to take away your sins and give you eternal life, you **belong** to Jesus forever. Forever never ends. And **Jesus wants you to enjoy your forever relationship with Him.**

If you have put your faith in Christ and trusted Him with your life, are you confident now that you are Jesus' sheep forever?

I hope you are confident. Jesus knows you by name. He calls to you, not so that you hear it in your ears but so that you hear it in your heart. He speaks to you as you read the Bible. The words in the Bible are His words to you. The sheep hear the Good Shepherd's voice and know it is true. Our hearts tell us to listen to Jesus and follow Him because He can be trusted.

Is this your response to Jesus as your shepherd? Do you want this to be your response?

DEEPER DISCOVERIES (OPTIONAL):

Spend a few minutes each day reading the verses below and reflecting on Jesus—His life, His relationships, and His teaching. Get to know Him well—this One who loves you dearly.

Read John 9:1-12. Reflect on what you read.

Read John 9:13-41. Reflect on what you read.

Read John 10:1-21. Reflect on what you read.

Read John 10:22-42. Reflect on what you read.

Jesus Is the Resurrection & the Life

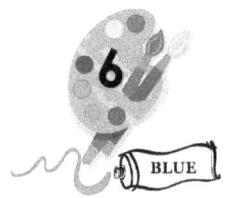

*Jesus said to her, **"I am the resurrection and the life.** The one who believes in me will live, even though they die; and whoever lives by believing in me will never die. Do you believe this?" (John 11:25-26)*

> **Pray:** Lord Jesus, please teach me through this lesson.

PAINTING THE PORTRAIT OF JESUS

- ✓ JESUS IS THE "I AM." He is the answer to the spiritual needs of every person. *John 8:58*

- ✓ JESUS IS THE BREAD OF LIFE. His abundant love satisfies our hunger for a relationship with God. *John 6:35*

- ✓ JESUS IS THE LIGHT OF THE WORLD. His light directs us to follow Him. *John 8:12*

- ✓ JESUS IS THE GATE FOR THE SHEEP. There is safety in following Jesus and doing life His way. *John 10:7, 9*

- ✓ JESUS IS THE GOOD SHEPHERD. You can enjoy a forever relationship with Him. *John 10:11, 14*

PAINT COLOR #6: BLUE

Our color for this lesson is blue.

When you think of things that are blue, what comes to mind?

Blue sometimes refers to a feeling of sadness. Have you ever heard someone say, "I'm feeling blue today?" The phrase "feeling blue" goes back to a custom on sailing ships. When a captain or other important crewmember died during the ocean voyage, the ship would fly blue flags and paint a blue stripe along the outside wall of the ship as it sailed home. When the families on the shore saw that blue flag on the ship entering the harbor, many wondered if it was their loved one who died.

Blue has a happier meaning, though. In the Bible, the color blue is a heavenly color. God told His people to make the curtains in the Tabernacle and the Temple out of fabric woven with blue, purple and scarlet yarn (Exodus 26; 2 Chronicles 3). When the prophet Ezekiel had a vision of God in heaven (Ezekiel 1:26), he saw God sitting on a blue colored throne. So, blue reminds us of being with God in heaven. As we have already learned, our life with God is called **eternal life**.

So, the color blue will represent for us **"the hope of eternal life."**

If someone very close to you became sick and died, how did that make you feel?

When you hear about someone dying, does that make you afraid about what might happen to you when you die?

Jesus understands the hurt we feel when someone close to us dies. He also understands our fears about death itself. He makes a wonderful promise to His followers about life and death. Let's find out what that is.

Jesus had 3 special friends—Lazarus and his two sisters, Martha and Mary. One day Lazarus became sick. By the time Jesus arrived in Bethany, Lazarus had already been dead and in the tomb for four days. He was very definitely dead, not just sleeping.

Read John 11:17-27.

When Martha discovered that Jesus was close by, what did she initially do and say (vv. 20-22)?

How did Jesus answer her (v. 23)?

What did Jesus declare to her in vv. 25-26?

How did Martha answer Jesus' question, "Do you believe this?"

Read John 11:28-35.

What happened next (vv. 28-32)?

How did Jesus respond when he saw Mary's pain (vv. 33, 35)?

Death of someone you love is usually a very sad thing. Jesus cried alongside His friends Mary & Martha. His heart was deeply moved and troubled by their pain. It provoked Him to share their sadness.

Read John 11:38-45.

The sisters took Jesus to Lazarus's tomb, and He said to remove the stone. In vv. 40-41, what did Jesus do and say?

After His prayer, what happened to Lazarus (vv. 43-44)?

Imagine the joy that followed that event.

How do you think Mary and Martha felt?

How do you think Lazarus felt?

How did the onlookers respond (v. 45)?

One thing we know, everyone in that town was talking about it. As a result of this incredible miracle, many people started believing in Jesus.

WHAT HAPPENS AT THE DEATH OF A BELIEVER

Look back at what Jesus told Martha about Himself, "I am the resurrection and the life (vv. 25-26)."

What does He promise to those who believe in Him?

When Jesus promised life, He was referring to **eternal life.** The Bible tells us that your soul goes to heaven to live with Jesus instantly after your body dies. Who you are on the inside will continue to live on with God in heaven. When you as a Christian die, it will be as though you go to sleep in this body and wake up in heaven with Jesus. Do you feel confident that this will happen to you?

FOLLOWING JESUS

Read Psalm 30:11-12.

How do these verses relate to our hope of heaven?

The word "resurrection" always refers to a dead person receiving a new physical body that will never die again. Lazarus was not resurrected. He was given a healed body but not a new body that would never die again. Lazarus' body died later on, just like everyone else who has lived on the earth.

Jesus was the first person ever **resurrected** from the dead. On the third day after His body died, God raised Him up from the dead and gave Him a brand-new body that would never die again. His new body was the same in many ways as His old body. It was human, could be seen and touched, could walk and talk, and could eat food.

Jesus' body was also different in that He didn't look exactly the same, He could appear and disappear in rooms without going through the doors, and He could not be hurt or sick anymore.

After Jesus spent 40 days on earth in His new resurrected human body, He left the earth to live in heaven. Today, He is sitting in heaven next to God the Father in His perfect human body. When you go to heaven and see Jesus, He will be human just like you and I are. He has two arms to hold you. He has two eyes to see you. Isn't that delightful?

Jesus goes on to say that after your body dies you will be very much alive and can never die again. That's because God will give you a new resurrected body just like Jesus' resurrected body that can never die again. It's a promise.

Jesus is the resurrection and the life. He gives to His followers eternal spiritual life now and eternal physical life in a new resurrected body after death.

Eternal life begins the moment we believe that Jesus is the Son of God and trust in Him to take away our sins. It's yours now. It's eternal because it is God's life living in you. Forever.

This is our hope. All humans need hope. You should feel confident in your spiritual life now and your future eternal physical life in a new resurrected body.

What do you think it will be like to have a resurrected body like Jesus' body?

*This is the **hope** of our future. Isn't that a wonderful promise? Nothing is too difficult for God to do!*

We can be joyful now about this hope. We can look forward to dancing with joy one day in heaven.

Pray: *Thank Jesus for His wonderful plan that takes away the fear of death.*

DEEPER DISCOVERIES (OPTIONAL):

Spend a few minutes each day reading the verses below and reflecting on Jesus—His life, His relationships, and His teaching. Get to know Him well—this One who loves you dearly.

Read John 11:1-37. Reflect on what you read.

Read John 11:38-57. Reflect on what you read.

Read John 12:1-19. Reflect on what you read.

Read John 12:20-50. Reflect on what you read.

Jesus Is the Way, the Truth & the Life

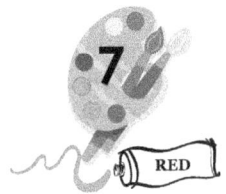

*Jesus answered, "**I am the way and the truth and the life.** No one comes to the Father except through me." (John 14:6)*

> **Pray:** Lord Jesus, please teach me through this lesson.

PAINTING THE PORTRAIT OF JESUS

- ✓ JESUS IS THE "I AM." He is the answer to the spiritual needs of every person. *John 8:58*

- ✓ JESUS IS THE BREAD OF LIFE. His abundant love satisfies our hunger for a relationship with God. *John 6:35*

- ✓ JESUS IS THE LIGHT OF THE WORLD. His light directs us to follow Him. *John 8:12*

- ✓ JESUS IS THE GATE FOR THE SHEEP. There is safety in following Jesus and doing life His way. *John 10:7, 9*

- ✓ JESUS IS THE GOOD SHEPHERD. You can enjoy a forever relationship with Him. *John 10:11, 14*

- ✓ JESUS IS THE RESURRECTION AND THE LIFE. To His followers, He gives eternal spiritual life now and eternal physical life in a new body after death. *John 10:25-26*

PAINT COLOR #7: RED

Our color for today is red. Many people like red as a favorite color. It's a bright color. Red is also the color that alerts you to danger. Flashing red lights at railroad crossings, red stoplights, and red stop signs all signal that the setting could be dangerous if you don't watch out. You need to stop whatever you are doing to avoid the danger. Sometimes in the Bible, red is used for the color of sin. That's God's way of saying sin is dangerous.

Red has some positive meanings, too. It is the color of **love**. Around Valentines' Day, red hearts are everywhere because red hearts represent love. Red is also the color of **life**. Blood is red; blood represents life. Without blood, we die. The American Red Cross is an organization that helps people during disasters. In fact, it is the largest supplier of blood and blood products in the United States. Its symbol is a red cross that represents blood as the gift of life.

In the Bible, the color red often connects **love** and **life** as it represents God's promise to His people to forgive their sins when a blood sacrifice was made. God made the promise because He loves us and wants to give us spiritual life that lasts forever.

Red is also the color of **celebration**. Sometimes a red carpet is rolled out on special occasions so the people walking along it feel special and important.

So, we'll say that red represents **love, life**, and **celebration**. Knowing how much we are embraced by God's love for us and receiving Jesus' life given to us now is certainly cause for celebration, isn't it? Anticipating our life in heaven one day is also a cause for celebration.

> *"In the same way, I tell you, there is rejoicing in the presence of the angels of God over one sinner who repents." (Luke 15:10)*

Read John 14:1-6.

> ***Jesus talked with His disciples about heaven. What did Jesus tell His disciples about where He was going (v. 2)?***

> ***What did He promise (v. 3)?***

He told them that He was going there soon, and they could follow because they knew the way to get there. But Thomas wasn't so sure about this.

What did Thomas say to Jesus (v. 5)?

What was Jesus' answer to Thomas and everyone else (v. 6)?

In this "I Am" statement, Jesus said He was three things—the way, the truth, and the life.

> *Based upon what you have already learned, what did Jesus mean by that statement?*

We can confidently say this: Jesus is the **way** to know God as Father because He shows us the **truth** about God in His life, and He gives His **life** to anyone who believes in Him.

Knowing Jesus is the only way to have a relationship with God. That's the way to heaven.

Let's look at each one of those words—WAY, TRUTH, and LIFE.

Jesus is the WAY

Jesus is the way. The question to ask is, "What way?"

Reread John 14:6.

> *Jesus is the way to what?*

Jesus says He is the only way for any person to have a relationship with God the Heavenly Father. How? By believing in Jesus.

Read Acts 4:12.

What did Jesus' disciple Peter say about Jesus as the way to know God?

The first Christians were so convinced of Jesus being the only Way to know God and taught this truth everywhere so they were called "Followers of the Way." As a "Follower of the Way," the apostle Paul traveled all over his world preaching that Jesus is the Way to know God, the Way to receive forgiveness for your sins, and the Way to live a life that pleases God. To anyone who asked him, "How can I know God?" Paul would answer, "Believe in the Lord Jesus Christ." He's the Way.

Based on this understanding, would you identify yourself as a "Follower of the Way?"

Other people may try to tell you that there are many ways to get to heaven, not just one way. Or they might say there are other gods out there besides the God of the Bible.

But you can tell them only one man died on the cross to pay the penalty for our sins—Jesus. Only one man was ever resurrected from the dead with a new body that will never die again—Jesus. Only Jesus was truly God. Anyone who believes in Jesus can now have forgiveness of their sins and a relationship with God.

No other religious leader has ever been resurrected from the dead. They are all in their graves. Jesus is not in His grave. He was resurrected from the grave, given a new body, and is sitting in heaven on His throne as king of planet Earth ready to welcome you and me when we trust in Him.

Jesus is the only way for any person to have a relationship with God. You have to start with that and believe that. Jesus said He is the way. Jesus also said He is the truth.

Jesus is the TRUTH

After Jesus told His disciples that He was the way, the truth, and the life, the very next thing He said was very important.

Read John 14:7. See also v. 10.

What did Jesus tell the disciples?

Who is His Father?

Jesus goes on to say that anyone who has seen Him (Jesus) has seen God the Father (v. 9). When Jesus was on earth, He showed everyone what God was like. Jesus was loving and kind, showing us God is loving and kind. Jesus was always good showing us that God is always good. Jesus showed us that God answers prayer and that God hates sin. Jesus was the living truth of God.

Because Jesus is God, believing in Him is the way to have a relationship with God. You can't believe in any other famous name or any other religious person to have a relationship with the God of the Bible, the one true God. Only through believing in Jesus.

Read John 8:31-32.

What did Jesus tell those who were listening to Him?

Jesus was the truth of God back then and is still the truth of God. Truth never changes. Jesus is the truth. Jesus is also the life.

Jesus is the LIFE

Anyone who believes in Jesus not only has a relationship with God but also receives eternal life. Remember that we said eternal life starts the moment you believe in Jesus and lasts forever. It can never end, and no one can take it away from you. Great news!

Read Romans 8:11.

What is the promise?

Even though your body dies, your soul lives on in heaven where you will one day receive a brand-new body just like Jesus' new body, one that will never die again. That's eternal life. But when Jesus said He is the life, He meant even more than that.

Read Galatians 2:20.

From this verse, how is Jesus your life today?

As part of God's family, God's Spirit comes to live inside you. God's Holy Spirit gives to you the joyful life of Jesus.

FOLLOWING JESUS

God's Spirit enables you to live a life that pleases God your Father. He changes the way you think and feel to be more like the way Jesus thought and felt when He was on earth.

It's as though Jesus' life just bubbles up from inside of you so that everyone can see that you love Him.

You have become a child of God the Father, completely loved and accepted by Him. Isn't it a great thing to be so very loved and accepted by the God who made you?

Jesus is the way, the truth, and the life. Jesus gives us His life so that we are completely loved and accepted by God our Father. Celebrate!

Response in prayer & praise:

Use any creative means to express your celebration of Jesus' life in you—drawing, painting, prose, poetry, song, or prayer. An extra page is added at the end of this lesson for your creativity. ☺

Or you can pray the prayer below that celebrates Jesus as the Way, the Truth, and the Life:

How absolutely amazing is your loving plan, oh God, that takes care of my need to know you! Help me to hold onto the truth that Jesus is the only way to have a relationship with God as my Father. Help me to believe that I am truly your child, completely loved and accepted by you the moment I trusted in Jesus. Fill my heart with joy and celebration because Jesus' life is inside me.

Spend a few minutes each day reading the verses below and reflecting on Jesus—His life, His relationships, and His teaching. Get to know Him well—this One who loves you dearly.

Read John 13:1-17. Reflect on what you read.

Read John 13:18-38. Reflect on what you read.

Read John 14:1-14. Reflect on what you read.

Read John 14:15-31. Reflect on what you read.

Jesus Is the Vine

I am the vine; you are the branches. Whoever abides in me and I in him, he it is that bears much fruit, for apart from me you can do nothing. (John 15:5 ESV)

Pray: Lord Jesus, please teach me through this lesson.

PAINTING THE PORTRAIT OF JESUS

- ✓ JESUS IS THE "I AM." He is the answer to the spiritual needs of every person. *John 8:58*

- ✓ JESUS IS THE BREAD OF LIFE. His abundant love satisfies our hunger for a relationship with God. *John 6:35*

- ✓ JESUS IS THE LIGHT OF THE WORLD. His light directs us to follow Him. *John 8:12*

- ✓ JESUS IS THE GATE FOR THE SHEEP. There is safety in following Jesus and doing life His way. *John 10:7, 9*

- ✓ JESUS IS THE GOOD SHEPHERD. You can enjoy a forever relationship with Him. *John 10:11, 14*

- ✓ JESUS IS THE RESURRECTION AND THE LIFE. To His followers, He gives eternal spiritual life now and eternal physical life in a new body after death. *John 10:25-26*

- ✓ JESUS IS THE WAY, THE TRUTH, AND THE LIFE. He gives us His life so that we are completely loved and accepted by God our Father. Celebrate! *John 14:6*

PAINT COLOR #8: BROWN

Our last color is brown. Consider the things in nature that are brown such as dirt, tree trunks, dead leaves, and some animals. Good healthy dirt for growing lots of vegetables and flowers is usually a nice dark brown—sort of crumbly and not too hard. Great garden soil combines regular dirt plus compost, which is decomposed organic matter like leaves, grass clippings, or cow manure. Some call compost "brown gold." It is so valuable because it transforms the dirt in your garden into a "plant-growing machine." Suddenly your tomato plants are producing so many tomatoes you can't pick them fast enough. Flowers bloom continuously, and grapevines produce lots of grapes. When it comes to growing things, brown represents **nourishment to bear fruit**.

Read John 15:1-5.

What does Jesus call Himself in today's "I am" statement (v. 5)?

What does He call His followers?

What were the branches supposed to do (v. 5)?

This is a passage about fruitfulness, not salvation. The branches are not individual believers but are collectively all of Jesus' followers. We've learned that Jesus used images to describe Himself that the people listening to Him could readily understand—bread, light, shepherd, and now a vine. The Jews were familiar with vines. There were grapevines everywhere planted in rows on farms called vineyards. In the spring, the vinedresser props up the branches (lifts up and away) or trims the branches (prunes) so they will **bear more fruit**. If any branch gets bent or broken off from the vine, the vine wouldn't be able to produce grapes through that branch.

When you think about a vine and branches, the vine has its roots in the ground. It gets the nutrients it needs from the dirt and carries them to the branches connected to the vine. The vine **nourishes** or feeds the branches. It's easy to understand this image of Jesus giving life to His followers. Jesus is referring to the spiritual life He gives to believers now while they are alive on earth. That life inside of us should bear Jesus fruit in our lives. The purpose of the vine is to **bear fruit** through its branches. Jesus chooses to **bear fruit** through His followers.

Think about how fruit is produced on a vine. In the spring, the vine wakes up from its winter's sleep and first grows new leaves on its branches. Pretty soon, flowers appear on those branches. Then, in a wonderful way, the flowers are transformed into tiny fruit that keep growing all summer long until they are ripe for picking. The vine has done what it is supposed to do—give **nourishment** to all its branches so they can **bear the fruit** the vine wants to produce on them.

You know the kind of vine that you are growing by its fruit. You would pluck grapes from a grapevine, kiwi fruit from a kiwi vine, and blackberries from a blackberry vine. So, the fruit should match the vine. That's what Jesus is saying about His followers, also. Their lives should match the kind of vine they are attached to—a Jesus vine. Anything that looks like what Jesus did when He was here on earth would be Jesus fruit. Jesus produces fruit through those who trust in Him and are His followers—the branches of His vine. Let's talk about what Jesus fruit would look like.

Jesus loved people. What would that kind of Jesus fruit look like in you?

Jesus talked to God His Father in prayer often, asking God to do whatever God wanted in His life. What would that kind of Jesus fruit look like in you?

Jesus spent time reading and studying God's word in the Bible He had, believing it and obeying it. What would that kind of Jesus fruit look like in you?

Jesus fruit in you is you looking more like Him in how you live your life every day. Jesus lived His life to please God His Father (John 8:29).

Jesus fruit in you can be seen as you live your life to please God your Father. There's a key to doing this. Look at our verse again.

Reread John 15:5.

What must we as Jesus followers do in order to bear Jesus fruit in our lives?

Why?

The "apart from me you can do nothing" in this verse refers to bearing Jesus fruit—living your life so that whatever you do or say looks more like what Jesus would do or say. Then people could say, "Hey, I can see that you are like Jesus."

The world will try to convince you that you've got power within yourself to do a lot of great things without relying on Jesus to do it through you. You can run a marathon on your two feet without being attached to the Jesus vine. You can do hundreds of math calculations without Jesus. You can be a top salesperson without Jesus. But you can't love people as Jesus loved them. You can't trust in God as Jesus trusted in God. You can't understand the Bible and obey it as Jesus did. You can't live your life to please God as Jesus did. You can do none of those things without receiving something from the Jesus vine. Jesus said to His followers, "You need something from me continually. You've got to remain connected to me."

What do you think it means to abide or remain (NIV) in Jesus?

First, let's talk about what that cannot mean. We have already learned that once you trust in Jesus to take away your sin, you have a forever relationship with Him that can never be taken away or lost. You have eternal life that begins now and continues forever that doesn't stop. And the Holy Spirit comes to live inside you forever. You cannot become "unjoined" to Jesus and lose the life He's given to you. But your life can look to others as though you are not connected to Him.

The word "abide" (or, remain) in this verse means to "dwell" in a certain place, to "make one's home" in that certain place or with that certain person. To remain in Jesus is to "make our home" in Him, just as He also "makes His home" in us.

Think about your home, the place where you live. What are the benefits of having a place to call home?

What makes it special to you?

Home is where you can relax, where your family is, where you feel loved, and where all the things that are truly important to you are. Home is where you get **nourished** with food and sleep so that you have the strength and encouragement to make it through the next day. It's where you learn how to grow up and live life that is worthwhile. Even when you are at work or school, you are still connected to your home. If you share your home with others, they are likely thinking about you and caring for you when you are away.

That's what Jesus wants to be for you as His follower—your home, your dwelling place. Not a building like a house, but you abide in a relationship like you have with a loving family at home. And it's in that relationship that we grow as branches and **bear Jesus fruit** in our lives. Not by ourselves, of course, for we have the Holy Spirit within us doing that, nourishing us with Jesus' life.

What would it look like for you to abide in Jesus?

FOLLOWING JESUS

When you trust in Jesus Christ to take away your sins, His Spirit comes to live inside of you. You can't see Him, but He is there from the moment you trust in Jesus. His job is to help you bear Jesus fruit so that you look more like Jesus in what you do and say every day. That's His job.

The Bible says that the Holy Spirit transforms you to become more and more like Jesus, just like the life of the vine transforms the flowers into fruit that represents the vine. You begin to look like you are attached to the Jesus vine, bearing Jesus fruit in your life.

The Bible describes some of that Jesus fruit in Galatians 5.

Read Galatians 5:22-23.

What kind of Jesus fruit does the Holy Spirit work to produce in a Christian's life?

All of the fruit in that list were produced in Jesus' life when He was on earth. He wants to produce this same fruit in your life. If you have these characteristics in your life, others will recognize that you are connected to the Jesus vine and that the Holy Spirit inside you is **nourishing** you with Jesus' life to transform you into someone who looks like Jesus in whatever you do and say.

One famous teacher put it this way:

> "Jesus Christ gave His life for you so that He could give His life to you so that He could live His life through you." (Ian Thomas, *The Saving Life of Christ*)

Read John 15:8.

When we bear Jesus fruit, who is honored?

This honors our Father God and pleases Him. You as a person always please God because you are His child. But what you do (attitudes, thoughts, words, actions) may not always please God. As you bear Jesus fruit, though, your life will please God every day.

Jesus is the vine. He nourishes us with His life so we can bear fruit in our lives that represents our connection with Him.

Recognize that you can do nothing that pleases God apart from Jesus. Nothing on your own. You need nourishment from Jesus to live a life that pleases God and bears Jesus fruit.

> **Pray:** *Thank Jesus that He nourishes you with His life so that you can bear Jesus fruit for Him. Tell Jesus that you choose to stay closely connected to Him through depending on Him to live His life through you.*

DEEPER DISCOVERIES (OPTIONAL):

Spend a few minutes each day reading the verses below and reflecting on Jesus—His life, His relationships, and His teaching. Get to know Him well—this One who loves you dearly.

Read John chapter 15. Reflect on what you read.

Read John chapter 16. Reflect on what you read.

Read John chapter 17. Reflect on what you read.

Read John chapter 18. Reflect on what you read.

Read John chapter 19. Reflect on what you read.

Read John chapter 20. Reflect on what you read.

Read John chapter 21. Reflect on what you read.

Sources

1. Ian Thomas, *The Saving Life of Christ*

2. Robert Deffinbaugh, That You Might Believe: A Study of the Gospel of John," posted on Bible.org

3. Tim Stevenson, "The Seven Great 'I Am's'" sermon series, 1998

4. Walvoord and Zuck, *The Bible Knowledge Commentary, New Testament*

5. William McDowell, "You Are God Alone" lyrics